THE BEST NBA
DUNKERS
OF ALL TIME

By Barry Wilner

www.abdopublishing.com

Published by Abdo Publishing, a division of ABDO, PO Box 398166, Minneapolis, Minnesota 55439. Copyright © 2015 by Abdo Consulting Group, Inc. International copyrights reserved in all countries. No part of this book may be reproduced in any form without written permission from the publisher. SportsZone™ is a trademark and logo of Abdo Publishing.

Printed in the United States of America, North Mankato, Minnesota
042014
092014

Cover Photos: John Swart/AP Images (left);
Alex Brandon/AP Images (right)
Interior Photos: John Swart/AP Images, 1 (left), 31; Alex Brandon/
AP Images, 1 (right); AP Images, 7, 9, 11, 15, 17, 25, 29; David Smith/
AP Images, 13; Lennox McLendon/AP Images, 19; Kevin Reece/Icon
SMI, 21; Rusty Kennedy/AP Images, 23; John Bazemore/AP Images, 27;
Michael Tweed/AP Images, 33; Kirthmon Dozier/AP Images, 35; Beth A.
Kaiser/AP Images, 37; David Tulis/Bettmann/CORBIS, 39; Jeff Haynes/
Newscom, 41; Pat Sullivan/AP Images, 43, 55; Elaine Thompson/AP
Images, 45; Dusan Vranic/AP Images, 47; Bill Kostroun/AP Images, 49;
Wilfredo Lee/AP Images, 51; Frank Franklin II/AP Images, 53; Eric Gay/
AP Images, 57; Mark J. Terrill/AP Images, 59, 61

Editor: Chrös McDougall
Series Designer: Christa Schneider

Library of Congress Control Number: 2014932902

Cataloging-in-Publication Data
Wilner, Barry.
 The best NBA dunkers of all time / Barry Wilner.
  p. cm. -- (NBA's best ever)
ISBN 978-1-62403-410-7
1. National Basketball Association--Juvenile literature. 2. Dunkers
(Basketball)--Juvenile literature.   I. Title.
796.323--dc23

2014932902

TABLE OF CONTENTS

INTRODUCTION

Through the years, slam dunks have been called many things. Throw-downs. Jams. Slams. Tomahawks.

Regardless of the name, nothing gets National Basketball Association (NBA) fans out of their seats like a jaw-dropping slam dunk from an amazing athlete. Some dunkers are famous for their air. They take off far away from the basket and glide through the air. Other players dunk with power. They slam the ball through the hoop. Then there are the tricksters. They leap into the air and move the ball up and down, side to side, and even between their legs. It does not matter the style, though. The dunk is often a surefire way for a player to score an exciting two points.

Here are some of the best dunkers in NBA history.

WILT CHAMBERLAIN

Wilt Chamberlain was nicknamed "The Big Dipper." He could also have been called "The Big Dunker." The center stood at 7 feet 1 inch and weighed 275 pounds. He towered over opponents throughout his 14-year NBA career. And he was a force when he got close to the hoop. It was almost impossible to stop the Big Dipper from dunking the ball.

Chamberlain was already huge in college. And he was already dominant. His University of Kansas teammates knew they just had to toss the ball near the rim. If it was close, Chamberlain could redirect the shot for a dunk. Both college basketball and the NBA banned those types of plays because of Chamberlain. It was one of many rules changed to slow "Wilt the Stilt."

Philadelphia Warriors center Wilt Chamberlain scores his 3,000th point of the 1961–62 season on a dunk.

Another such rule change widened the foul lane. This forced centers to cover more ground to get to the basket. NBA players also were formerly allowed to take a running start on free throws. But that stopped after Chamberlain did so and dunked a free throw.

The rule changes did not matter, though. Chamberlain could not be stopped. He led the NBA in scoring in each of his first seven seasons in the NBA. Plus he had the league's best field-goal percentage an amazing nine times. That is because so many of his shots were dunks.

Chamberlain's most incredible moment came on March 2, 1962, in Hershey, Pennsylvania. That night he scored 100 points against the New York Knicks. It remains an NBA record by a long shot. And the last of Chamberlain's 36 baskets came on a "Dipper Dunk."

100

The number of points Wilt Chamberlain scored in one game in 1962. It was still an NBA record through 2013.

The Los Angeles Lakers' Wilt Chamberlain dunks against the New York Knicks during a 1972 playoff game.

WILT CHAMBERLAIN

Position: Center

Hometown: Philadelphia, Pennsylvania

College: University of Kansas

Height, Weight: 7 feet 1, 275 pounds

Birth Date: August 21, 1936

Teams: Philadelphia/San Francisco Warriors (1959–65)
  Philadelphia 76ers (1965–68)
  Los Angeles Lakers (1968–73)

All-Star Games: 13 (1960–69, 1971–73)

MVP Awards: 1959–60, 1965–66, 1966–67, 1967–68

First-Team All-NBA: 1959–60, 1960–61, 1961–62, 1963–64,
  1965–66, 1966–67, 1967–68

CONNIE HAWKINS

Basketball is known as a street game.
And no one was a better street baller than Connie
Hawkins. He had long arms and huge hands. When he
leapt into the air, he could spin and twist his body. Fans
would take subways and buses to different New York
City parks to see "The Hawk" play.

The Harlem Globetrotters noticed Hawkins's
dunks, too. Hawkins ended up playing for the famous
exhibition team for parts of four years. His calling card
was dunking.

Those dunks began when Hawkins was in grade
school. He first dunked at age 11. But he did not play
organized ball until he was a high school junior. By his
senior year, he was an All-American. Hawkins could
shoot well from as far out as 20 feet (6.01 m). But
what most people remember him for was how well he
threw down.

Phoenix Suns forward Connie Hawkins flies past a Philadelphia
76ers defender to the hoop during a 1969 game.

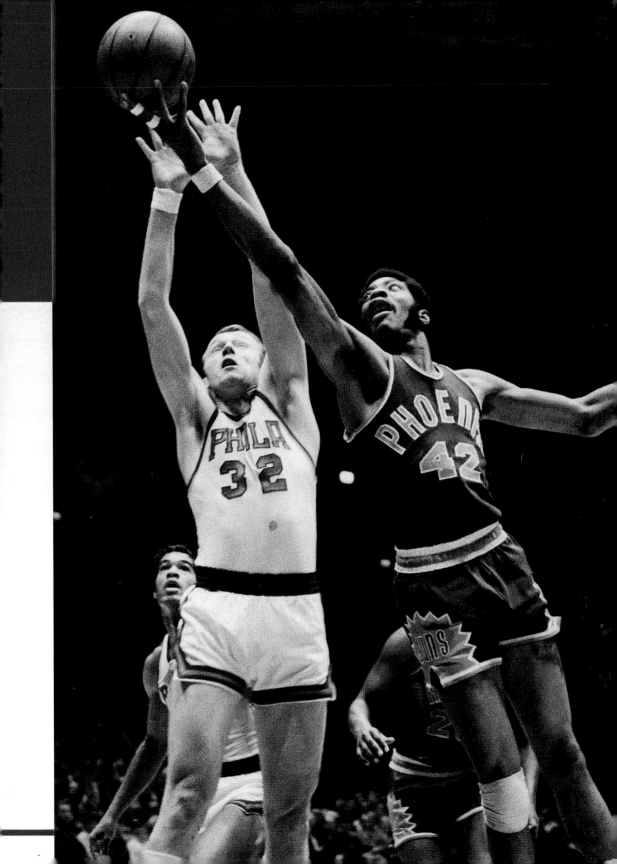

Hawkins modeled his game after that of Los Angeles Lakers star Elgin Baylor.

"I think he was the first guy I'd ever seen who had that certain flair for the game," Hawkins said. "I adapted my game after his. See, once you learn to play in the schoolyard, you can almost adapt your game to anything."

Hawkins's journey to the NBA was long. He spent a short time at the University of Iowa. Then he joined the Globetrotters. After that, he joined the American Basketball Association (ABA). That was a rival league to the NBA. Two seasons later, in 1969, Hawkins finally joined the NBA's Phoenix Suns. And his dunks certainly made him memorable once he got there. Hawkins played a total of nine seasons in the ABA and the NBA. Later he was inducted into the Basketball Hall of Fame.

789, 603

The number of free throws Connie Hawkins attempted and made as an ABA rookie in 1967–68. Both were league highs.

Connie Hawkins was one of the ABA's and NBA's great dunkers in the 1960s and 1970s.

CONNIE HAWKINS

Position: Forward

Hometown: New York, New York

College: University of Iowa

Height, Weight: 6 feet 8, 210 pounds

Birth Date: July 17, 1942

Teams: Pittsburgh Pipers/Minnesota Pipers (1967–69)*;
Phoenix Suns (1969–73); Los Angeles Lakers
(1973–75); Atlanta Hawks (1975–76)

All-Star Games: 5 (1968, 1970–73)*

First-Team All-NBA: 1967–68, 1968–69, 1969–70*

* Stats from 1969 and earlier are from the ABA.

JULIUS ERVING

Julius "Dr. J" Erving does not own any real medical degrees. He certainly knew how to operate around the basket, though.

Erving first became a superstar in the ABA. The ABA merged with the NBA in 1976. By then, Erving was already a legend. Dr. J won three league Most Valuable Player (MVP) Awards. But he was best known for his amazing dunks.

The ABA always fought an uphill battle against the older, richer NBA. But it had its share of stars. And the league made efforts to highlight those stars. One way it did that was through a dunk contest. The ABA introduced the event during its 1976 All-Star Game in Denver. And it had a perfect centerpiece.

Philadelphia 76ers forward Julius Erving throws down a dunk against the Portland Trail Blazers in the 1977 NBA Finals.

Dr. J was known for dunking from all angles. He seemed to fly through the air on his way to the hoop. Erving took that skill to a new level at the first dunk contest. He was up against other great dunkers in Artis Gilmore, Larry Kenon, George Gervin, and David "Skywalker" Thompson. Each player had to do five dunks in two minutes. And the dunks had to be done from different parts of the floor.

Erving was a strong favorite. When it was his turn, the other All-Stars gathered to watch from the sidelines. Erving and Thompson matched spectacular dunk after spectacular dunk. But then Thompson missed one. And Erving erased all doubts about who was the king of dunks. He actually had a name for his final throw down: the "Iron Cross." Erving stretched his right arm far from his body while palming the ball. The rest of his body floated toward the basket. *SLAM.*

16

The number of All-Star Games in which Julius Erving appeared during his 16 professional seasons. He was the NBA All-Star Game MVP in 1977 and 1983.

Julius Erving of the 76ers was known for his ability to soar through the air for dunks.

JULIUS ERVING

Position: Small forward

Hometown: Roosevelt, New York

College: University of Massachusetts

Height, Weight: 6 feet 6, 200 pounds

Birth Date: February 22, 1950

Teams: Virginia Squires (1971–73); New York
Nets (1973–76)*; Philadelphia 76ers (1976–87)

All-Star Games: 16 (1972–87)*

MVP Awards: 1973–74, 1974–75, 1975–76, 1980–81*

First-Team All-NBA: 1972–73, 1973–74, 1974–75, 1975–76,
1977–78, 1979–80, 1980–81, 1981–82, 1982–83*

Slam Dunk Contest wins: 1976*

* Stats from 1976 and earlier are from the ABA.

DAVID THOMPSON

Luke Skywalker became a science fiction icon when the first Star Wars movie came out in 1977. He was not the first Skywalker, though. David Thompson had the name first. It was a fitting nickname for one of the greatest leapers in basketball history.

Thompson stood at 6 feet 4 inches. But he could out-jump players who were half a foot taller. In fact, Thompson could jump so high that he could touch the top of the backboard. "Skywalker" was also fast. His first step to the basket was so quick that he often left defenders flat-footed.

Thompson could thrive without dunking, too. Dunking was outlawed when he played college basketball. Officials worried that dunking was dangerous and damaged the hoops. Thompson had a good backup plan.

Denver Nuggets forward David Thompson sets up for a dunk during a 1976 game against the New York Nets.

Instead of dunking, Thompson lightly dropped the ball into the hoop. Those baskets helped his North Carolina State University Wolfpack win the 1974 national title.

Skywalker was ready to get to the pros and start dunking. He started his pro career in the dunk-happy ABA. He could do a lot with his 44-inch (1.12 m) vertical leap. Thompson would often slam the ball with his elbow high above the rim.

One of Thompson's greatest games came as the 1977–78 season ended. He was battling San Antonio Spurs guard George Gervin for the NBA scoring title. One afternoon, Thompson soared for 73 points. Only Wilt Chamberlain had scored more in one game at the time. Thompson's dunks that day made all the highlight reels. He did not win the scoring title, though. Gervin scored 63 that night to beat him out. Still, that did little to tarnish Thompson's Hall of Fame career.

126.48

The Denver Nuggets' points per game average with David Thompson during the 1981–82 season. It was still an NBA record through 2013.

David Thompson threw down some massive dunks during his Hall of Fame career.

DAVID THOMPSON

Position: Forward-Guard

Hometown: Shelby, North Carolina

College: North Carolina State University

Height, Weight: 6 feet 4, 195 pounds

Birth Date: July 13, 1954

Teams: Denver Nuggets (1975–82)*
  Seattle SuperSonics (1982–84)

All-Star Games: 5 (1976–79, 1983)*

First-Team All-NBA: 1976–77, 1977–78
* Stats from 1976 and earlier are from the ABA.

DARRYL DAWKINS

He was tall. He was wide. And he had a huge smile. Darryl Dawkins referred to himself as "Chocolate Thunder." That was also the name of one of his famous slam dunks.

Dawkins did not just lay down amazing dunks. He also gave his slams fun names. There was the "In-Your-Face Disgrace." Or the "Look Out Below." How about "Rim-Wrecker." "Go-Rilla." "Spine Chiller Supreme." "Cover Your Head." The longest name might have been the "Get out the wayin', back-door swayin', game delayin', if you ain't groovin' you best get movin' dunk."

Dawkins shared all these names through his wide grin. The creativity seemed fitting for a guy who claimed to come from the planet Lovetron.

Philadelphia 76ers center Darryl Dawkins follows through with a dunk during a 1980 playoff game against the Atlanta Hawks.

Dawkins joined the Philadelphia 76ers in 1975. He was one of the first players drafted directly from high school. His game was all power. Often that meant mighty jams.

The 76ers were playing the Kansas City Kings in 1979. Dawkins headed to the basket. But Bill Robinzine was in his way. No worries. Dawkins went up and over Robinzine and threw down the ball. And down came a shattered backboard. Even Dawkins was stunned at what he had done.

Yet a few weeks later, Dawkins went in for another jam in a home gam . The backboard again broke. This time, even the rim came down—intact. If Dawkins never again dunked, he would already have earned his fame. But, of course, he slammed and jammed many more times in his career. And the NBA responded by installing new shatterproof baskets and breakaway rims in every arena.

18

The age at which Darryl Dawkins made his NBA debut. He did not score a point in his first three games with the Philadelphia 76ers.

The backboard shatters after the 76ers' Darryl Dawkins threw down a massive dunk in 1979.

DARRYL DAWKINS

Position: Center

Hometown: Orlando, Florida

High School: Evans High School

Height, Weight: 6 feet 11, 251 pounds

Birth Date: January 11, 1957

Teams: Philadelphia 76ers (1975–82)
New Jersey Nets (1982–86)
Utah Jazz (1987)
Detroit Pistons (1987–89)

DOMINIQUE WILKINS

The NBA introduced a Slam Dunk Contest in 1984. Fans today still talk of the 1988 contest. It was a showdown between two of the greatest dunkers of all time: Michael Jordan and Dominique Wilkins. Wilkins had won the contest in 1985. Jordan had taken the title in 1987. The 1988 All-Star Game was at Jordan's home arena in Chicago. And he challenged Wilkins to a showdown.

"Expectations in Chicago are out of this world," Wilkins said.

The contest came down to the final round. Combined, the two superstars put down six dunks. Four of them scored a perfect 50. But many believe it should have been five. Wilkins had an impressive two-handed windmill jam. Jordan said he would have given it a 50. The judges scored it 45. "I was shocked," Jordan said.

Atlanta Hawks forward Dominique Wilkins was one of the NBA's most powerful dunkers during his 15 NBA seasons.

Jordan went on to win the contest with an iconic dunk. He took off from the free-throw line and slammed home the winner. Fifty points. Wilkins could only shake his head and smile.

Jordan went on to more fame. But many believe Wilkins to be the better dunker. He had long arms to help him throw down. And he dunked with grace, skill, and power. Fans began calling Wilkins the "Human Highlight Film."

Wilkins played most of his career with the Atlanta Hawks. The forward also nicknamed "Nique" was one of the NBA's best players during his 11-plus seasons there. He made the All-Star Game nine times for the Hawks. He also went on to win the 1990 dunk contest. However, Wilkins is most often remembered for his 1988 showdown with Jordan.

30.3

Dominique Wilkins's NBA-leading points per game average in 1985–86. Wilkins was the NBA's last scoring champion before Michael Jordan won seven in a row.

The Hawks' Dominique Wilkins dunks against the Boston Celtics during a 1988 playoff game.

DOMINIQUE WILKINS

Position: Small forward

Hometown: Washington, North Carolina

College: University of Georgia

Height, Weight: 6 feet 7, 200 pounds

Birth Date: January 12, 1960

Teams: Atlanta Hawks (1982–94)
Los Angeles Clippers (1994)
Boston Celtics (1994–95)
San Antonio Spurs (1996–97)
Orlando Magic (1999)

All-Star Games: 9 (1986–94)

First-Team All-NBA: 1985–86

Slam Dunk Contest wins: 1985, 1990

CLYDE
DREXLER

Clyde "The Glide" Drexler was best known for two things. One was running the floor on fast breaks. The other was dunking.

Drexler played basketball for the University of Houston. His high-flying team was nicknamed Phi Slamma Jamma. And Drexler brought that wide-open, break-for-the-hoop style to the NBA in 1983.

Drexler played most of his career with the Portland Trail Blazers. In 1992, the Blazers reached the NBA Finals. Michael Jordan and his Chicago Bulls won the series. But it was Drexler who threw down the Finals' most memorable dunk.

The Portland Trail Blazers' Clyde Drexler goes up for a dunk against the Chicago Bulls during the 1992 NBA Finals.

It was in Game 2. The play began when Drexler drove to the basket. His shot was blocked, though. Up the court came the Bulls. But Portland stole the ball. This time, Drexler did more than glide to the basket. He took a pass and drove right at Bulls center Bill Cartwright. Cartwright was six inches taller and 35 pounds heavier than Drexler. But that did not stop him.

Drexler soared into the air. Then he dunked right over Cartwright. He also got fouled. Drexler slowly walked to the free throw line. There was no taunting. No big celebration. Drexler never even looked back at Cartwright. That was the kind of player Drexler was— smooth, graceful, exciting, and often spectacular. But he was all business, all the time.

Drexler's childhood idol was Julius Erving. Growing up, Drexler would try to mimic Erving. He would do windmills and tomahawk dunks and reverses. Years later, Erving made the introduction when Drexler entered the Hall of Fame.

2,207

Drexler's steals in his career, many of which led to basket-shaking slams.

Clyde Drexler of the Houston Rockets sails above a Los Angeles Clippers defender in 1997.

CLYDE DREXLER

Position: Forward-Guard

Hometown: Houston, Texas

College: University of Houston

Height, Weight: 6 feet 7, 210 pounds

Birth Date: June 22, 1962

Teams: Portland Trail Blazers (1983–95)
Houston Rockets (1995–98)

All-Star Games: 10 (1986, 1988–94, 1996–97)

First-Team All-NBA: 1991–92

MICHAEL JORDAN

Some players use the dunk to show off their grace and athletic skills. Others throw down to display their power. And others still like the dunk because it is the highest-percentage shot in basketball. For Michael Jordan, the dunk was all about intimidation.

The shooting guard played most of his career with the Chicago Bulls. Many consider him to be the best to ever play the game. Jordan had quickness. He had strength. He had smarts. He could do just about everything—on offense and defense. What made him great, however, was his approach to the game. Jordan struck fear into opponents. One way he did that was by jamming over and through them.

Chicago Bulls guard Michael Jordan wows the fans with a high-flying jam at the 1988 Slam Dunk Contest.

Jordan showed his skills in winning the 1987 and 1988 Slam Dunk Contests. But he also showed that one of his fierce slams could change a game. That is exactly what he did in 1991. The Bulls were on their way to the team's first NBA championship.

They stopped in New York to play the rival Knicks. At one point during the game, Jordan dribbled along the baseline on the left side of the court. Then he did a half-spin and leaped toward the basket. In his way was 7-foot center Patrick Ewing.

Ewing was a great defender. But Jordan did not care. He rose up and threw down over Ewing's outstretched arms. The play also drew a foul. After the play, a Knicks television analyst said, "This is an ego problem for Patrick Ewing." It was just the message Jordan was delivering. He did that to everyone. No wonder he led the Bulls to six NBA titles in eight seasons.

6

The number of NBA Finals MVP Awards Michael Jordan won during his career. That was twice as many as any other player through 2013.

The Bulls' Michael Jordan dunks against the Indiana Pacers during a 1998 playoff game.

MICHAEL JORDAN

Position: Shooting guard

Hometown: Wilmington, North Carolina

College: University of North Carolina

Height, Weight: 6 feet 6, 195 pounds

Birth Date: February 17, 1963

Teams: Chicago Bulls (1984–93, 1995–98)
Washington Wizards (2001–03)

All-Star Games: 14 (1985–93, 1996–98, 2002–03)

MVP Awards: 1987–88, 1990–91, 1991–92, 1995–96, 1997–98

First-Team All-NBA: 1986–87, 1987–88, 1988–89, 1989–90, 1990–91, 1991–92, 1992–93, 1995–96, 1996–97, 1997–98

Slam Dunk Contest wins: 1987, 1988

SPUD WEBB

NBA teammates used to tease Spud Webb. They would say he was in the wrong sport. They said at 5 feet 6 inches, he should be a jockey. Then they saw how Webb could dunk.

At first glance, Webb looked out of place. It was the 1986 Slam Dunk Contest. Out came spectacular dunkers such as Dominique Wilkins. And then there was Webb. All of the other players towered over him. But the little point guard was out to prove himself in his hometown of Dallas.

Webb indeed got all the way to the final round. But there he faced his Atlanta Hawks teammate Wilkins. The forward stood more than a foot taller than Webb. He was also the defending champion of the dunk contest. But Webb was not afraid.

Atlanta Hawks guard Spud Webb challenges Boston Celtics forward Larry Bird during a 1988 game.

On one dunk, the ball hit his head as it fell through the netting. Another was a double clutch two-hander. Then he dunked after a full spin-around. The clincher came when Webb began by bouncing the ball off the floor. It then bounced off the backboard. Finally, Webb grabbed it and slammed it through the hoop. That gave him the win. Three of Webb's dunks that day even received perfect scores.

Webb was an outstanding NBA point guard for 12 seasons. He had a quick first step and good dribbling skills. Plus he was a sharp passer. Sure, a few more inches might have helped his game. But his fast hands and feet still made him a strong defender. What people most remember about Webb, though, was his dunking. And in 2011 at age 47, Webb showed he could still dunk. He even did it while wearing business clothes.

66

Spud Webb's height in inches. He stood 54 inches below the rim.

Spud Webb, *right*, and Michael Jordan, two of the NBA's most famous dunkers, judge the 2003 Slam Dunk Contest.

SPUD WEBB

Position: Point guard

Hometown: Dallas, Texas

College: North Carolina State University

Height, Weight: 5 feet 6, 133 pounds

Birth Date: July 13, 1963

Teams: Atlanta Hawks (1985–91, 1995–96)
Sacramento Kings (1991–95)
Minnesota Timberwolves (1996)
Orlando Magic (1998)

Slam Dunk Contest wins: 1986

SHAWN KEMP

Point guard Gary Payton had a secret weapon when he wanted an easy assist. All he had to do was throw up a high pass. Seattle SuperSonics teammate Shawn Kemp would then slam it down for an alley-oop. Together, the duo helped make the Sonics one of the best NBA teams of the 1990s.

Kemp was a big guy at 6 feet 10 inches. Yet the athletic forward flew through the air like he was a bird. He seemed to leap as high as the backboard. And he loved to hang on the rim after a dunk and enjoy it. It was as if he was at home up there during his 14 NBA seasons.

"The best feeling is when you dunk on a big guy bigger than you," Kemp said. "Then you can give him that look. It shrinks him down a bit. You're not quite 7 foot any more."

Seattle SuperSonics forward Shawn Kemp goes up for a dunk against the Houston Rockets in a 1997 playoff game.

Kemp never won the Slam Dunk Contest. But he always was one of the players to beat. And he took more pride in his dunks during games because they were not rehearsed.

The highlight reel of Kemp's dunks seems never ending. One memorable jam came at Madison Square Garden. New York Knicks forward Kenny "Sky" Walker was a great leaper himself. But Kemp dunked over him.

Former teammate Nate McMillan used to lob the ball high in the air for Kemp. The "Reign Man," as Kemp was called, would then grab the ball and hammer it into the hoop.

"It was fun," McMillan said. "He was an entertainer."

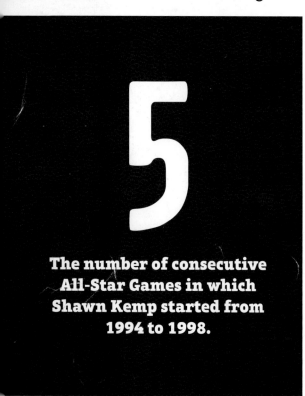

5

The number of consecutive All-Star Games in which Shawn Kemp started from 1994 to 1998.

Shawn Kemp sometimes seemed to spend more time in the air than on the ground for the SuperSonics.

SHAWN KEMP

Position: Power forward

Hometown: Elkhart, Indiana

College: Trinity Valley (Texas) Community College

Height, Weight: 6 feet 10, 230 pounds

Birth Date: November 26, 1969

Teams: Seattle SuperSonics (1989–97)
    Cleveland Cavaliers (1997–2000)
    Portland Trail Blazers (2000–02)
    Orlando Magic (2002–03)

All-Star Games: 6 (1993–98)

VINCE CARTER

Vince Carter joined the NBA in 1999.
NBA fans quickly got used to seeing his high-flying jams. One season later, he won the Slam Dunk Contest. And the following summer as a member of the US Olympic team, he took his high-flying ways global.

It was the 2000 Olympic Games in Sydney, Australia. Carter and Team USA were playing France. Carter stole a pass, and only France center Frederic Weis stood between him and the hoop. Weis stood 7 feet 2 inches tall. But Carter was not afraid. He took two dribbles and launched himself into the air.

Carter could have driven into Weis and hoped for a foul. That was not his style, though. Instead, Carter leapt straight over Weis. He closed out the play by slamming the ball through the hoop.

Team USA's Vince Carter dunks over 7-footer Frederic Weis of France at the 2000 Olympics.

Carter could embarrass anyone with his dunking skills. This one was special, though. The fans in the arena leaped to their feet cheering. They knew they would likely never see another slam like this one. Carter looked up to the ceiling. Then he pumped his right arm.

Teammate Kevin Garnett gave Carter a friendly little shove. Carter then stepped back and pumped both arms while throwing out his chest.

"That's one dunk, when I see it on tape, I actually want to rewind because I want to see it again," Carter said.

Carter has thrown down many memorable dunks in his career. In 2013–14, he began his sixteenth season in the NBA.

2001

Vince Carter's graduating class at the University of North Carolina. He left school after his junior year in 1998 but kept taking classes. Carter attended his graduation ceremony even though he had a playoff game that night.

Vince Carter of the New Jersey Nets dunks over the Indiana Pacers in the 2006 playoffs.

VINCE CARTER

Position: Guard-Forward

Hometown: Daytona Beach, Florida

College: University of North Carolina

Height, Weight: 6 feet 6, 215 pounds

Birth Date: January 26, 1977

Teams: Toronto Raptors (1999–2004)
New Jersey Nets (2004–09)
Orlando Magic (2009–10)
Phoenix Suns (2010–11)
Dallas Mavericks (2011–)

All-Star Games: 8 (2000–07)

Slam Dunk Contest wins: 2000

LeBRON JAMES

LeBron James is not often accused of being one-dimensional. The man nicknamed "King James" can do it all. And he can do just about everything really, really well. He can shoot, pass, rebound, defend, and lead. Those skills helped him win four NBA MVP Awards in five years. But perhaps the most exciting part of his game is his monster dunks.

James is 6 feet 8 inches and supremely athletic. He uses his big body not only to throw down but also to intimidate. That showed during one 2013 game. James and his Miami Heat teammates were trailing the Boston Celtics by 13 points. Then Heat guard Dwyane Wade stole the ball and passed it to teammate Mario Chalmers. Chalmers immediately passed it to Norris Cole, who then passed to James. The big forward finished the play with a backboard-shaking dunk.

Miami Heat forward LeBron James dunks against the Boston Celtics during a 2013 game.

Boston guard Jason Terry fell to the floor on the play. Afterward, James stared down Terry. The taunt resulted in a technical foul. But James thought it was worth it.

"It's one of my better ones," James said, "and the fact that it happened to J. T. makes it even that much sweeter, because we all know J. T. talks too much sometimes."

King James has dunked on just about everyone in basketball. He did it as a teenager. James won the McDonald's Slam Dunk Contest in high school. He did it in the NBA. And he did it in three Olympic Games for Team USA. But he does not like dunk contests.

"I'm more of an in-game dunker," he said.

Just ask Terry.

500

The number of consecutive regular-season games in which LeBron James scored at least 10 points after he dropped 35 on the Toronto Raptors on November 5, 2013.

The Heat's LeBron James throws down a dunk against the New York Knicks during a 2014 game.

LeBRON JAMES

Position: Forward

Hometown: Akron, Ohio

High School: Saint Vincent-Saint Mary

Height, Weight: 6 feet 8, 240 pounds

Birth Date: December 30, 1984

Teams: Cleveland Cavaliers (2003–10)
Miami Heat (2010–)

All-Star Games: 10 (2005–14)

MVP Awards: 2008–09, 2009–10, 2011–12, 2012–13

First-Team All-NBA: 2005–06, 2007–08, 2008–09, 2009–10,
2010–11, 2011–12, 2012–13

DWIGHT HOWARD

The Orlando Magic drafted Dwight Howard straight out of high school. As such, the big center was very raw. There was one area that he had already mastered, though. Howard could slam it home like the best of them.

Howard's nickname is "Superman." It is a fitting nickname for a player who can fly through the air. And after throwing down, Howard loves to flex his muscles.

Howard's dunking ability has helped make him an NBA superstar. And along the way, he has dunked over some of the NBA's biggest names. His slams against superstars Kobe Bryant and Tim Duncan are among his most famous. The slam over Duncan came in the last second of the game off a long in-bounds pass, and it won the game.

Houston Rockets center Dwight Howard dunks against the Cleveland Cavaliers during a 2014 game.

In 2008, Howard showed he was the king of dunks in the Slam Dunk Contest. The showstopper came on his second dunk. He grabbed a Superman cape. Then he got a running start and took off from the free-throw line. Meanwhile, a partner had thrown the ball off the backboard. Howard caught the ball mid-air and threw it through the hoop.

Howard sealed the win with his second-to-last dunk. He lobbed the ball into the air. Then he jumped. Mid-air, he tapped the ball off the backboard with his left hand, and then dunked with his right hand. The TV announcers called it humanly impossible. But it was not impossible for Superman.

5

The number of consecutive seasons in which Dwight Howard led the NBA in total rebounds, from 2005–06 to 2009–10.

NBA All-Star Saturday Night

Wearing a Superman costume, Dwight Howard soars to the hoop during the 2008 Slam Dunk Contest.

DWIGHT HOWARD

Position: Center

Hometown: Atlanta, Georgia

High School: Southwest Atlanta Christian

Height, Weight: 6 feet 11, 240 pounds

Birth Date: December 8, 1985

Teams: Orlando Magic (2004–12); Los Angeles Lakers (2012–13); Houston Rockets (2013–)

All-Star Games: 8 (2007–14)

First-Team All-NBA: 2007-08, 2008-09, 2009-10, 2010-11, 2011-12

Slam Dunk Contest wins: 2008

BLAKE GRIFFIN

The Los Angeles Clippers picked Blake Griffin first overall in the 2009 NBA Draft. The young forward was eager to start his professional career. But then he broke his left kneecap in a preseason game. He never saw the court that season.

Griffin quickly made up for lost time. He debuted during the 2010–11 season. And he did so with one amazing dunk after another. Sometimes it seemed the backboard would collapse from the power of his jams. But he also had an artist's touch.

The 2011 Slam Dunk Contest was on Griffin's home court. The local star was the favorite over DeMar DeRozan, Serge Ibaka, and Javale McGee. But Griffin knew he had to get creative to satisfy the home crowd. So he called in a choir.

Los Angeles Clippers power forward Blake Griffin rises for a jam against the Los Angeles Lakers in 2014.

The choir began belting out the song "I Believe I Can Fly." That is when Griffin took a pass from teammate Baron Davis. Where was Davis? He was sitting inside a Kia Optima automobile on the court. Davis passed the ball up through the open sunroof. Griffin caught the ball as he leaped over the car and then dunked.

That iconic dunk put Griffin on the map. But his big-time jams are hardly limited to dunk contests. The powerful forward is known for his ability to fly through the air. Once he takes flight, he is nearly impossible to stop.

In fact, the Clippers have made Griffin's dunks a big part of their offense. Point guard Chris Paul throws up passes. Griffin throws them down. It is no surprise that fans have nicknamed the Clippers "Lob City."

270

The total number of offensive rebounds Blake Griffin had in 2010–11. He won the NBA's Rookie of the Year Award that season.

Blake Griffin dunks over a Kia Optima during the 2011 Slam Dunk Contest.

BLAKE GRIFFIN

Position: Power forward

Hometown: Edmond, Oklahoma

College: University of Oklahoma

Height, Weight: 6 feet 10, 251 pounds

Birth Date: March 16, 1989

Team: Los Angeles Clippers (2010–)

All-Star Games: 4 (2011–14)

Slam Dunk Contest wins: 2011

HONORABLE MENTIONS

Kobe Bryant – The Los Angeles Lakers' star is a lights-out shooter, but he is also known for his ability to drive to the hoop and throw down. He won the 1997 Slam Dunk Contest.

Gorilla – Have you ever seen a gorilla flying through a flaming hoop on the way to a dunk? The Phoenix Suns' mascot, "The Gorilla," does just that. Even the players often stop to watch his performances.

Gerald Green – Coming straight from high school to the NBA was tough for Green. But the guy can sure dunk. The 2007 Slam Dunk Contest champion famously set a cupcake on the rim and blew out the candle while competing in the 2008 Dunk Contest.

Gus Johnson – No one was more exciting on the fast break during the 1960s and early 1970s. "Honeycomb" was the best player from Akron, Ohio, until LeBron James came along.

Larry Nance – Winner of the first NBA Slam Dunk Contest in 1984, Nance was known for getting his elbows above the rim before slamming.

Jason Richardson – A two-time Slam Dunk Contest winner (2002 and 2003), Richardson became known for the "Up And Under." He threw the ball off the backboard, caught it, put it between his legs, and then slammed it home.

Nate Robinson – Anyone measuring 5-foot-9 who can win three Slam Dunk Contests (2006, 2009, and 2010) and throw down with guys a foot taller is sure to get noticed.

Dwyane Wade – No one was quicker to the hoop than Wade in his early pro seasons. His high-flying dunks helped him lead his Miami Heat to three NBA championships through 2013.

GLOSSARY

alley-oop
A dunk in which a player catches a pass in the air and dunks the ball.

assist
A pass that leads directly to a basket.

blocked shot
A play in which a shooter's field goal attempt is knocked down by a defender before it can reach the rim.

clutch
A fake in which the player pulls the ball back.

draft
A system used by leagues to spread incoming talent throughout all of the teams.

rookie
A first-year player in the NBA.

tomahawk
A type of dunk in which the player slams the ball through the hoop with his arm extended.

windmill
A type of dunk in which the player takes a long windup before slamming the ball through the hoop.

FOR MORE INFORMATION

Further Readings

Silverman, Drew. *Basketball.* Minneapolis, MN: Abdo Publishing Co., 2012.

Silverman, Drew. *The NBA Finals.* Minneapolis, MN: Abdo Publishing Co., 2013.

Stoudemire, Amar'e. *Slam Dunk.* New York: Scholastic Press, 2013.

Websites

To learn more about NBA's Best Ever, visit **booklinks.abdopublishing.com.** These links are routinely monitored and updated to provide the most current information available.

INDEX

ABOUT THE AUTHOR

Barry Wilner has been a sportswriter for The Associated Press since 1976. He has written about every sport and has covered every Super Bowl since 1985. He has also covered every World Cup since 1986, the Stanley Cup Finals, the Olympic Games, the Pan American Games, championship boxing matches, and major golf and tennis tournaments. Wilner has written more than 40 books.